MW01282034

"RAISING A PRINCE WITHOUT A KING"

A Single Mother's Journey To Victory

LaVeda M. Jones

Love Clones Publishing
www.lcpublishing.net

Copyright © 2015 by LaVeda Jones. All rights reserved. This book or any portion thereof may not be reproduced or used in any manner whatsoever without the express written permission of the publisher except for the use of brief quotations in a book review.

Printed in the United States of America

First Printing, 2015

ISBN: 978-0-692-39124-2

King James Version
Scripture quotations marked "KJV" are taken from the Holy Bible, King James Version (Public Domain).

New King James Version
Scripture quotations marked "NKJV" are taken from the New King James Version. Copyright © 1982 by Thomas Nelson, Inc. Used by permission. All rights reserved.

New American Standard Bible
Scripture quotations marked "NASB" are taken from the New American Standard Bible®, Copyright © 1960, 1962, 1963, 1968, 1971, 1972, 1973, 1975, 1977, 1995 by The Lockman Foundation. Used by permission.

Publishers:
Love Clones Publishing
Dallas, TX 75205
www.lcpublishing.net

ENDORSEMENTS

"As ministers who come into daily contact with single moms, my wife and I are proud to endorse this work by LaVeda M. Jones. The task of raising males in today's society can be daunting, but with God's grace, as demonstrated so beautifully in this book, the impossible becomes possible!" - **Reverend and Mrs. Thomas Patrick O'Connor**

"LaVeda Jones is a woman who thankfully has listened to God's calling and is making a difference in this world. Her message is one that resonates to any single parent, young or old. The story she has shared is only the beginning. Her influence, support and gift of encouragement, strength, love and faith that God is working for us - is comforting and so needed. LaVeda has a gift, is a gift and thankfully God is moving in her, through her and with her every step of the way." – **Christine Welch, Owner, Coffee Cake Connection**

"LaVeda Jones, a woman of faith, is deeply committed to the health, happiness and wellbeing of her family and boys. This book is symbolic of her commitment and journey...focused and goal oriented. It is a love letter to those who may traverse parenthood without a partner, so that they know they are not alone. With God as your guide and a spiritual foundation, all things are possible." - **Yolanda Daniel, Global Business and Finance Executive**

"*Every child at some time in his or her life has dreamed of what he or she wants life to be as an adult. For various reasons that perfect dream is shattered. Hence, Raising a Prince Without A King, born out of a dream deferred, LaVeda Jones shares the real struggles of a single parent raising children alone in a way that encourages one to continue on in the struggle. You will laugh. You will cry. You will be encouraged!* "– **Apostle Deborah Stackhouse, The Sign of the Dove Church**

"*Raising children is never an easy task and parenting as a single adult can present greater challenges. The testimony found in these pages will not only encourage you but leave you feeling hopeful and refreshed. I believe that through the transparency of her personal journey, Laveda Jones has written a book full of the healing power of God. This is definitely a must read for all single parents!*"– ***Pastor Carla Walker, Cathedral of Power International***

DEDICATION

This book is dedicated to my God "Dad" Arthur B. Hearn (1926-2014). You embraced me, educated me, taught me, trained me, guided me and most of all, you loved me. Every valuable lesson is stored and remembered in my heart. I am humbled to have had you a part of my life, not every young girl is blessed to have a Dad as amazing, braved, intelligent, gentle, kind and a superhero like you.

As the tears roll down my faced typing this note, I am encouraged to know that you were a gift from my Heavenly Father and although you were taken so abruptly from my life, you will remain in my heart and your legacy will live on. I hold tight to all the laughs, travels, phone calls, hugs and kisses you gracefully gave me each and every time we were together. Thank you for teaching me to stand tall when things got rough, how to groom my boys' hair, how to love and forgive and how to be a blessing to those less fortunate than me. I hope I have made you proud. As I continue to follow God's mission for my life I promise to carry your legacy everywhere I go. I love you "Daddy".

WORDS FROM MY CHILDREN

My Dearest Mom,

    I want to start off by saying how proud I am of you. You don't allow anything to stop you from reaching your goals. This is not always easy but you sure make it look as though it is through your faith in God. I've watched you prosper and it only gets greater as the years pass on. It has captured my attention so much, that I now try to mimic it through my life goals. You are very inspiring, motivating and I will always love you for that so thank you so much. – Love you, Beverly Early, Your Baby girl

Mom,

    Mom you've raised me as a single mother for 14 years. Some people might think that it's really hard, but for you Mom it isn't. Even though you have raised me alone you still manage to get me the things that I want and need. I know you struggle sometimes, but God keeps on blessing you so that we may have food to eat, a house to live in and clothes to wear. Thank you Mom for going out of the way for me even when you have no money, you still make a way for us. I know you do these things for us so we are always reminded that you want us to have the best life. I've seen obstacles come your way, but you never let anything stop you. There are times we get on your last nerves but you still love us. You may be a single mother but you're the best mother I could ever ask for. – Love you Mommy from Noah Polk

Mommy,

I love you and thank you for being the best Mommy. You always take care of me and I never want to live without you. – Love Nathaniel "Nate" Polk

ACKNOWLDGEMENTS

Having now authored my first book, it is imperative for me to acknowledge all the amazing people in my life who prayed with me, taught me, influenced and blessed me.

To my Mother, Frances Jones, thank you for life, teaching me valuable lessons about parenting and how to turn two nickels into a dollar. You have encouraged me continual through the years with your support and love. Your teachings will be with me always and I value you as a mother.

To my Father Johnny Jones and Step-Mother Ruthie Jones, you are amazing parents and I am blessed to have you in my life. Thank you for you love, support and being a true example of what leaders, parents and children of God should be.

To my loving and adorable children, Beverly Early, Noah Polk and Nathaniel Polk, I have learned to love without boundaries and inspired to be the best I can be for each of you. Through your love, patience and support I have committed my life to be a positive role model and a mother that will not only parent you, but listen, understand and teach you the way through the word of God. Each of you has given me so much to be thankful for. As I chase my dreams, my prayer is that you never stop dreaming and believing dreams can come true. Hold fast to God's unchanging hands and trust that He is the only way and the one to follow. Thank you, my babies for being incredible and easy to love.

To my siblings, Cathy Jones, Thomas Jones, Valerie Jones, Shanice Gipson, Antoinette Smalls, Angela Jones, Johnny Jones, Jr., Regina Jones, Kimberly Rhodes, William Jones, Cassandra Maynard-Knighten and Darryl Maynard, each of you have a special place in my heart and my love for you continues to grow daily. Thank you for your encouragement.

To my in-laws Mr. Anthony Polk, Theresa Polk and Antoinette Polk thank you for your support, love and care. You have instilled family values into the boy's lives that they will always treasure. We are blessed to have you as family.

To Noriel and Trasa Noriega and family thank you for stepping up as Godparents in our time of need. You gave, shared and provided security in our lives when we felt hopeless and because of your continued love we thrived and are bless to have you a part of our lives.

To my grandmother, all my aunts, uncles, nieces, nephews, cousins and family I love you all and each of you has crafted me to be the woman I am today.

To my Apostles and spiritual parents Harry and Deborah Stackhouse, words can't express my gratitude for you. Your prayers, love, embrace and teachings have transformed me into the person I am today. You have challenged me to progress to the next level and trained me to be all that I can be. You have guided me when I felt lost and mentored me so I would win.

To Pastors Chris and Carla Walker, just thinking about what you mean to me and how you have encouraged me to press when I felt hopeless about publishing this book, my heart is overwhelmed and grateful to have friends like you. Thank you both for believing in me and loving me the way you do.

To Pastors Douglas and Chere Nabor, only God could have brought you and used you in my life the way He did. Thank you for taken a chance with me and giving me an opportunity to use my gifts and talents in your ministry. Thank you for opening your lives up to us. I will forever be grateful.

To my dearest friends, Demetria Waddell, Crystal Elliott-O'Connor, Neshelle Kaiser, Janece Jenkins, Danetta Collins, Kimberly Collins, Nicole Craig, Linda Scott, Rochelle Wilson, NiQuita Hampton, Julienne King, Malika Cox, Aaron Cole, Devalyn Golliday, Geneace Williams, Robert Johnson, Sundrea

Richardson, Claudette Thomas, Debbie Randle, Betty Phillips, LaVetta Bunch, Mother Sutton, LaJune Jones, Keesha Currington, Timberlain Woodruff and Kimberlain Woodruff-Smith, without each of you I wouldn't be where I am today.

To my dearest Amber Collins, you have been my rock and support for many years. You have taught me gentleness, love and respect. Thank you for being supportive, steadfast, and lovable.

To my best buddy and friend Terry Heights, thank you for being a true friend and always standing by my side. I could not have made this journey without your friendship and support during the most critical times in my life.

I take this time to say to each of you, thank you and I love you.

TABLE OF CONTENTS

FOREWORD

In this masterfully written book LaVeda Jones addresses the problem of single motherhood with insight and candor. In her relaxed gentle style she takes us on an emotional rollercoaster that most single mothers experience. This book is about a woman who suffered dashed hope, failure, fear, the absence of peace, the squashing of self-confidence, the abandoning of friends, to a woman rising from the ashes to becoming person of strength, faith and courage.

In her darkest times and deepest fears she ultimately came to the conclusion that what she needed to direct her life and raise her children was a blueprint from God.

The book chronicles her dreams of being a happily married woman working from home raising her children, to the divorce that devastated her life leaving her gripped with the reality that she had to go the distance of child raising alone. With a child in each of her arms and hope in the promises of God in her heart, she navigated life's waters of uncertainty to the shores of success.

I have had the privilege of knowing Laveda and her two sons Noah and Nate for three years. My wife, Deborah, and I have made them part of our family.

"Raising a Prince Without a King" is LaVeda Jones' story on pages. What you will read is exactly what she lives.

LaVeda is an excellent mother who has raised her boys in the admonition of the Lord. She sought the Lord's direction on how to raise them, and step by step and through His guidance she has nurtured two wonderful sons into well-grounded, confident, talented princes.

This book is a testament to the grace of God and the determination of a woman who was willing to put her trust in the Lord. The psalmist said in Psalm 56:3-4 *"When I am afraid, I will put my trust in You, in God, whose word I praise, in God I have put my trust, I shall not be afraid..."* NAS

Apostle Harry Stackhouse
The Sign of the Dove Church, Waukegan, IL

PREFACE

The story you are about to read is my journey of victory as a single mother and not to be confused or compared to others. This is my story. I am grateful to The Father for embracing me and teaching me about the fruit of the spirit. *But the Holy Spirit produces this kind of fruit in our lives: love, joy, peace, patience, kindness, goodness, faithfulness, gentleness, and self-control. There is no law against these things. (Galatians 5:22-23 NLT)*

As a child I'd never daydreamed about being a single mother. Actually I'm reminded by my Mother that I wanted to have all the children in the world while working as a veterinarian and living in a mansion with my husband. I have always loved children and animals and thought having them in my life would bring me comfort. I'm so glad that was only a childhood fantasy. Maybe unconsciously, I knew single parenting was tough because I watched my Mother struggle with in it all my life, caring and providing for our family. Sharing a three bedroom with three siblings and one cousin was rough. As a teen the sibling number grew to five and we had to share everything. From food, clothes, shoes, money and we had to minimize asking for new things because my Mother couldn't afford it. My Mother was a seamstress so we were blessed to have personalized designer jeans and dresses by FMJ my Mother Frances M. Jones (should this be explained); they were not Jordache Jeans or Cheryl Tiegs dresses but they were beautiful and tailored to fit each of us perfectly.

I appreciate the sacrifices my Mother made to make our lives comfortable. However, I never desired to repeat her struggles. I once thought single parenting was her choice until I got older. I wanted my Mother to marry and she didn't. I always questioned as a child if she enjoyed the struggle or just didn't care about being single. To my surprise I was wrong, she did have a choice. Although my choice was much different from my Mother's, it led me to the same road of single parenting.

So while I have your attention may this book inspire you to never give up and to trust that God will provide. No matter what you are facing, tomorrow is coming with new grace and mercy.

CHAPTER ONE

WHEN YOUR PLANS FAIL

For I know the plans I have for you," declares the LORD, "plans to prosper you and not to harm you, plans to give you hope and a future.

Jeremiah 29:11

Oh, how wonderful it was the day I held him in my arms. I looked into his big bright eyes and promised him the world. I imagined the perfect life for the three of us. The big house with a swing set, working from home, and anticipating daily when I would hear his precious footsteps running through the house greeting the love of my life at the front door with the aroma of dinner embracing him like a warm blanket. That's the life my child deserved and the life I dreamt of as a child.

After a year, my dreams were scattered. My hope for a perfect home was gone, and I was left alone to raise not only one son but now two without a father. Devastation engulfed my plans, circumstances detoured my path and fear gripped my mind. What will I do now, was the question that pondered my mind daily. I lost my peace, confidence, self esteem, friends, home, job and most of all the ability to stand strong. I had to learn to navigate my life with two children without a father and had very little optimism that my future would be greater than my past.

I found myself staring in the mirror on occasion wondering if the reflection staring back at me would ever stop crying and find hope again. I would change the expression on my face to see what worked best so I could learn to look different from the way I felt. No matter how I twisted my face nothing brought comfort to the deep unrepaired scar that wouldn't heal properly regardless of how I tried to aide it over and over again. So I discovered that a mask was the perfect solution to cover the scar from others as I learned the new route of my life.

When the phone would ring I had to strain to carry the conversation past one minute and if I got a visitor, I would excuse myself several times to run to the bathroom to wash the tears from my eyes. I never liked being invited to birthday parties because I had to endure the painful questions over and over again "So how are you? Have you heard from your ex? Is he still with the other woman? Can I do something to help?" I'm sure many of them were really sincere but to me just a hello and a hug would've been the ideal healing mechanism that I needed at that time. Nevertheless, my phone kept ringing, visitors kept coming and birthday invitations flooded my mail box. I eventually decided that something had to give.

Now I'm angry and my priorities were like a jig saw puzzle, and I wanted answers to my many questions of why me? I cried out to God "Can You hear my cry? I tried doing right, I feel so alone." I was consumed with my daily task and trying to figure out my new life as a single mother. I watched all my married friends prosper in their marriages as I saw my own life going up in flames. I wanted answers, I wanted help and I wanted to be loved again. At times I wanted to give up, I wanted to jump off the highest cliff and I didn't want to be me any longer. I kept looking for a change, staring yet again in the mirror hoping I would see a different reflection but nothing changed.

I could hear the depths of my heart crying for comfort in the middle of the night and there was no one there to hold me. I would wake constantly in fear from a nightmare that everything I dreamt of would never be accomplished and all that I thought of myself was only a vague memory with no lasting impact. I didn't know how to smile any longer and learning it again was too painful. It was easier to look hopeless and live out the definition, than to try and make all the muscles in my face cooperate with my thoughts just to please others. I didn't care what others thought or how they wanted me to be. I wanted to be left alone and vanish off the face of the earth.

The wounds were so deep that they penetrated the veins of my heart and occasionally I thought I would die of a heart attack or worse take my own life. I couldn't stop the pain, I couldn't fight any longer, and I couldn't breathe, I could only imagine. Imagine for a second that tomorrow could be better if I would try to figure out the next steps, plans and actions I needed to take for a brighter future. The more I tried focusing on tomorrow the more my eyes crossed, twitched, watered and rolled back in my head. Tomorrow in my reality wasn't worth focusing on; today was all I had to hold on to. Today I needed to figure out how to hug my boys and say the three most powerful words that would give them hope "I LOVE YOU", without breaking down.

Escaping the turmoil of my current situation was imperative and wrapping my thoughts around the possibility seemed like only a dream but something had to change and quickly. I could feel freedom trying to squeeze its way into my life bringing a sunrise without the dawn and a cool breeze without a chill but I couldn't reach out to grab hold. It seemed to be unreachable, far in the distance and intangible, like a whisper in the night that is so vague you wonder if you really heard it.

With my eyes closed and my lungs expanding to capture a fantasy that just wasn't enough, I needed a release. This hole I'd dug was deep and every attempt to discharge myself pushed me down deeper without the ability to grab and pull up. I remember the despaired feeling I had when I looked up and said a prayer: "Father God, I ask that you place your ear to my heart and not only hear my words but feel the vibration of every beat that fades daily with a hopeless tone. I am desperate and I need You to cradle me with security, love and most of all faith to believe and trust in you with everything and my children, amen.

That prayer was prayed as if it was my last echo of hope. And I needed my Father to rescue me because I had reached a place where my life was fading quickly. I had separated myself from people and those that were tangible didn't know how to help me. Keeping that distance between others and me made sense because I didn't have to pretend or mask my emotions. Although it felt right, emotionally I was dying inside. I knew that if I couldn't get the courage to cry out loud to my family and friends, I could cry out loud to God. It was like a sunken pit in my stomach, the pain was unbearable and just knowing tomorrow was coming and there was no change in my situation made my anxiety even greater.

On bended knees, as tears drenched my clothing, I released a loud cry of desperation. I felt that this was my only and final chance to be rescued. My thoughts had over taken my future; my pain had snatched my hope and tomorrow felt like a year away. I remember thinking that as broken as I am, there's only "One" who could help me. So I prayed and cried and prayed and cried until my body slowly collapsed to the floor with only a few breaths remaining I said "amen." I knew my night was complete as I lay in a puddle of tears anticipating if God heard me and what He would say.

As I closed my eyes, turned my face to the wall, exhaled a few times and listened to the fast beat of my heart, I knew I was incapable of helping myself. Although I struggled most of the night trying to find peace, I knew eventually it would be mine. I don't recall what I dreamt that night or even if I had a dream I only remember waking up feeling as though I'd wrestled throughout the night.

I was exhausted as I heard the cry of my oldest son from the other room that morning. It was time to mask yet again so I could properly care for my precious child. Holding all my emotions inward and placing a smile on my face. As I entered his room as a necessity, there he was with the biggest grin and arms raised above his head patiently waiting for his morning kiss and hug.

It wasn't easy masking my emotions with my son, although he could not express what he was feeling into a sentence, I believe he felt the disturbance from my spirit to his. He would gently lay his head on my shoulder and say I love you as though he knew those words would change me instantly. Instant restoration is what I needed and his soft whisper of love gave me the strength to progress and make the best of the day. Holding my child in my arms brought a soothing sensation to my mind that only the love of a little one can give. He was special and although my world was upside down he made the view of the impossible, possible.

I remember saying this would never happen to me...

CHAPTER TWO

WHEN THE UNEXPECTED HAPPENS

In the same way, the Spirit helps us in our weakness. We do not know what we ought to pray for, but the Spirit himself intercedes for us with groans that words cannot express.

Romans 8:26

It was unexpected. I never thought it would happen to me; just the thought of motherhood frightened me. I'm too young. I had a goal to become a famous singer maybe even a movie star and let's not forget about teaching art in as many states as possible before my departure from this world. I only had one month left before I walked the stage to receive my BFA in Visual Communications. We talked about getting married in the next couple of years after I landed my dream job and him going back to school to finish his degree. Having a family at this stage in our lives wasn't the right time at least that's what we thought.

After five pregnancy tests and that stomach dropping moment I felt right before I shared the BIG news, I balled my eyes out. I have disappointed God, my mother and myself. Over and over it played in my mind, you're no different now, you should've been more careful and what have you done? Just the thought of him leaving me or being alone was overwhelming. I waited until he arrived home and said guess what you're going to be a father.

I didn't get the reaction I planned for but I did get one. Our lives as we knew it were changing and we needed to make the right decision about our future quickly. Pondering how we would break the news to our folks brought on more anxiety and sickness than I could really handle but we had to tell them. Each family accepted the news the best way they could, considering the circumstances. Regardless of what poor decisions we as young adult parents made, a life was entering this world and we all had a responsibility to ensure this child was loved, cared for, and nurtured by each of us. We needed to put our emotions and frustrations in check, because regardless of anyone's approval this child was destined to arrive and would have an impact on us all so we needed to prepare to welcome him with open arms no matter what.

I recall searching for classes and trying to get as much wisdom and knowledge necessary to become a good mother to my child. I didn't want to make any mistakes. I was young and not necessarily ready, so educating myself became vital. I didn't know at the time, most of what I needed I already had and God would give the other things to me upon my baby's arrival. I had books, videos and a class to teach me everything. Being an exceptional parent was not only important to me, but it was who I felt I needed to become. I tried to overcompensate for those things I felt I lacked, hoping this child would view me as supermom with extraordinary powers to love him beyond measure.

My sweet, dear bouncing baby boy entered the
world on February 14th weighing 5 lbs. 14 oz. and 19
inches long. What a special Valentine's Day gift God
blessed us with! I recall this being the happiest
moment of my life. My handsome little baby boy was
perfect. His eyes were so bright and big as though he
could look deep into my heart and see the love I held
for him. I remember counting his toes and fingers and
thanking God for his health. I was in love for the first
time ever; this baby took me to a place emotionally I
had never experienced and it felt good. Just thinking
about it now brings goose bumps and tears because I
know from that moment forth I would love him deeply
and he would love me back.

A year later my love and I married. We were going
to be the perfect family. I had it all, a good job,
husband, son and nice living arrangements, what
more could I need. Everything seemed to be coming
together in spite of the past doubts, fears and
concerns I carried like a person weighed down with
baggage. I decided to bury them as though they never
happened and moved on. What I had at the moment
was the only thing that mattered to me, my family.
Being a good wife and mother consumed me but I had
to hide my faults. The things I battled within my mind
constantly took my happiness. I worried about

tomorrow every second and what if things didn't work.

Not very long after the great celebration and a few months of tough times my life as I knew it was turned upside down again; my love and I separated. Here I was with a toddler and pregnant with our second child. I started to question all my actions and even wondered if I was loveable or not. How could this be? Why did I ignore all the signs? What's wrong with me? Am I not pretty enough? Does he not love me? Tears flooded my pillow like a rainfall crashing into rocks. I was empty, troubled and feared my outcome. I wanted to murmur a prayer to God but I had turned away years prior and didn't know if He would hear my cry.

The stress of my life got the best of me. I had no energy and I was drained from the result of the life I thought was perfect. I created a world that wasn't real. There was clear evidence that the world I perceived to be perfect was only my imagination because the chaos in our home was served on a platter all day long. We argued, screamed and yelled at each other as though this was the norm. Our relationship was far from healthy and the best solution for us at that time was to separate.

With a new baby on the way, and making the decision to be apart was even harder to accept;

however, I couldn't bring another precious child into our world of pure madness. Although our decision to separate was hard on our toddler, I'd rather help him cope with the absence of his father than being caught in the middle heated arguments on a daily bases. It was not often that my husband and I could agree on much, but we did manage to think about our son and mutually agreed that the separation was the best option.

Hearing my son call for his dad daily was heartbreaking and having to tell your child daddy isn't here and probably won't come later was even worse. I would beat myself up because of the decisions I had made. Not once did we think about the children. We were selfish and had allowed our personal feelings toward one another to rule. I would love to blame the downfall of our marriage on my ex-husband but I played a part as well. Now my part wasn't as intense as his, but I played the role of defense. When you are hurting, the best way to respond to hurt is to hurt greater than the pain you feel. At least at that moment I thought that to be true. Many years later I realized that my defense mechanism was inappropriate and with my words, I had caused just as much pain to him as he had done to me.

Thinking about everything even now is

penetrating sadness to my heart because when we were in a heated moment we didn't realize the repercussion of our actions. If only I knew what I know now I'm sure our decisions would be a little different. I could easily blame our age as a factor to how we handled our disagreements or our marriage but the truth is we were self-absorbed. We wanted what we wanted and the cost of getting our way caused scars from wounds that may take a lifetime to heal.

The wedge we placed between our lives affected everyone around us. We never took into consideration that our attitudes, anger, bitterness and hatred would bring families and friends at war with one another. It's hard to maintain a good relationship with the in-laws and mutual friends when the person they love, you hate. I know hate is a harsh word but during that time that's how we felt about one another. It's weird how someone you loved and couldn't live without becomes someone you quickly dismiss and you wish you'd never met.

We would make one another smile without trying. We once were each other's best friend and living apart was never a thought. We had known one another for ten years before our first date. Who knew that the love we once had for each other could be so bad and almost destroy our future. I guess it's true what they say "There's a thin line between love a hate".

Although our love turned bitter, we were gifted with a precious child that brought us joy. The bond between the two of them was incredible. I remember watching him pace the floor with our baby in his arms in the middle of the night to comfort him. Sometimes he would sing to him and rub his brow softly and kiss his head. They loved one another, it was obvious and deep down inside it pained me because this is what I wanted for our family forever but because of self-addictions, lies and unfaithfulness the vision that should've remained, vanished.

Chapter Three

IT'S A MIRACLE

Answer me when I call to you, O my righteous God. Give me relief from my distress; be merciful to me and hear my prayer.

Psalm 4:1

I found myself gazing out the window early one morning smiling at what life was, and then crying at what life had become. I began reminiscing about the pregnancy of my youngest child and the long nine months of pain, fear and exhaustion as I carried him. I remember the day I found out I was pregnant. I was in total shock knowing that I had diligently taken precaution especially with a marriage going sour and a hopeless future with exceeding kinks that just couldn't be ironed out. Being pregnant at that moment wasn't the best timing. I contemplated daily on what I should do. I didn't think I had a connection with God any longer because I left Him for my mate. So, I felt as though His ears were closed to my prayers. I finally made the decision to carry and love my child regardless, but I was extremely emotional yet optimistic about our future.

Within the third month of my pregnancy I began having difficulties. The baby was laying on my sciatic nerve and my left side became immobile several times throughout the day. I was in excruciating pain daily for the remainder of the pregnancy. I had frequent visits to the chiropractor and my OB/GYN for help and support, but nothing seemed to work. I walked with a cane, crawled to the bathroom and couldn't stand for long periods of time. I knew then that this child was going to be special due to all the pain I was enduring. Thoughts raced through my mind if this baby would be smart, an inventor, athlete, minister or would he never want to leave home.

Once I hit my third trimester, I had my second ultrasound and I was excited to know that I was having another boy. Joy filled my heart to know that I would have two amazing and handsome men in my life to love me. As I was experiencing a joyful moment which wasn't frequent, I received a call from the doctor asking me to come for an appointment so I could speak with a specialist about the ultrasound. Once more, fear ran rampant through my mind; I just couldn't handle anything else. I reached out to my husband to ask him to escort me to the hospital, as the doctors needed us both to be present. We managed to agree and make this appointment together to learn the fate of our unborn child.

We made our way to the hospital to speak with the specialist to find out that my baby boy might have a birth defect and that he may not live more than 72 hours after delivery. The specialist asked us questions about our family history on each side to determine what could be the cause of the sudden change. Being raised by a single mother and not having any history on my father made my answer particularly difficult to answer. I started crying because I couldn't answer the questions and I felt embarrassed that I had no information about my biological father. This was just a reminder of how messed up my life had become. Here I was sitting in this room with a broken marriage, no background on my father to share with the specialist and getting the news that my precious child may not live. Shortly after my moment of a breakdown the specialist gave us a few options to consider and we needed to give an answer before leaving.

As tears rolled down my face and I looked her in her eyes she spoke these words " You can terminate the pregnancy because of the severity of the defect, get more testing done or do nothing and wait." We chose to do nothing but wait while praying. I knew that I needed to turn to God because He was my best and only option. I began praying and sending emails to everyone I knew that could pray because I needed a miracle.

We were asked to return to the hospital in three weeks to do one final ultrasound to see if things had changed. Those three weeks of waiting, crying and praying seemed like three months. The day arrived for me to see my doctor for one last ultrasound before delivery. I slowly walked in the room, sweating, praying and scared. I remember lying on the table with my eyes closed anticipating the words of my doctor. She finally spoke after about 15 minutes, "This can't be right, what we saw three weeks ago I no longer see". She called someone else to take a look as they compared the two ultrasounds. They were in awe. It was a miracle. God saved and healed my baby.

On September 20th my 6 lbs. 15 oz. and 21 ½ inch long baby boy was born. They laid him on my chest and I cried with joy. He made it through it all and God did it. I gave no one to credit for this miracle except for the one and only miracle maker. God proved to me that He still heard me and loved me deeply. Excitement flooded my heart to hold my miracle baby boy. I looked into his big brown eyes and named him and promised to love him forever with the best of my ability.

Just three weeks after my son was born I made the decision to relocate with the boys hundreds of miles away from family, friends and love ones. My family couldn't understand my decision and honestly I didn't either. I remember one evening I prayed this prayer "Lord God, if you have any plans for my life greater than what I am experiencing now, save me". I received confirmation after a long talk with my employer that I would relocate to Dallas, TX. After the long drive with two small children, I reached my new home. I wasn't sure what would happen to us or how things would turn out, but I trusted God, that this was the best option.

We spent exactly one year in Dallas. I was faced with many trials and concerns for my children being so far away from family, but I was desperate and had to take desperate measures to have peace. I was so tormented with my past and filled with anger that I had no choice or any other options, as least that's what I thought. Hatred gripped my heart and my imagination went wild and if I would've allowed my emotions to take over I would not be alive today. I had suicidal thoughts and I literally murdered people in my heart because of the anger that was stored within. I could not let go of the fact that this had happened to me. My life had been altered and I could not go back and change it.

I remember getting settled in my new place, a one bedroom, cute kitchen, living room and a pool off the back entrance. My oldest son slept in the top bunk; I slept in the bottom bunk and my baby in his crib. It was very intimate and it became my safe haven. There were many lonely nights and times I feared if I had made the right decision. The challenges of being away were tough because only my family and close friends knew where I was. I literally vanished in the sight of others; I cut off all communication for months because I didn't want to be persuaded to return home or have unexpected guest.

Night after night my heart boiled with separation anxiety, I needed my mother to hold me and tell me that everything was going to be ok. I needed my friends to come over and laugh with me and tell me everything was going to be ok. I needed my family to surround me with their love and tell me everything was going to be ok. I was scared and hopeless I didn't know how to fight through the sadness and fear of being all alone.

I remember receiving a call from my best buddy from college; he was currently living in Atlanta. He knew I had moved to Dallas but he didn't know the experiences I was facing and the hurt I was enduring but he knew to always call me on time. We came up with a plan of action to help me challenge my loneliness. We decided that every Friday night we would rent the same movie and order the same food and call each other on the phone and spend the evening together as if we were in the same place. We would laugh and he would let me cry without judging me and console me. For more than nine months he committed to being there for me.

After twelve months in Dallas I made the decision to return home, not knowing what to expect or how I would be received. Dallas taught me how to stand and press. Although my experience there was difficult, I knew returning home and facing what I'd ran from was the right thing to do. I also thought that I needed to give my children what I never had. My mother ran to Chicago after my birth and I never knew my father growing up. I didn't want to repeat the same behavior of my mother. Being a mother now, I understood why my mother reacted the way she did and her thoughts behind relocating, but it wasn't right. This was my chance to break the curse and allow my children to have a father and love him without boundaries, regardless of how I felt.

After 20 plus hours on the road with two small children we returned to Chicago. I was immediately embraced by my family. As I rested for a few hours I knew I needed to make a phone call that would change the course of my children's life. I needed to call their father. A few hours later he came over and my oldest son lit up and ran swiftly while calling "Daddy". My heart jumped with joy watching the two reunite. I knew at that moment I had made the right choice by returning home. My baby boy lay in my arms watching everything, I'm sure if he could communicate his words they would have been, "... And who is this, Mom?" as father and son's eyes connected they smiled and family happencd.

I would love to say we lived happily ever after, but that's not how the story ends. With a year separating our emotions we immediately wanted to reconnect. However, the reality was, life happened and we needed to accept things the way they were. Although we tried and considered on several occasions to make things work we knew the best options was for a divorce. We had to bring the two families back together and let go of the past regardless of how painful it was and allow healing to take place. After countless efforts, failures and emotions all over the place giving our children a fair chance to develop their own opinions and relationships was the right thing to do.

We had made enough mistakes and caused damage that only the Father could heal. It was time for us to become adults, grow up and make the right choices. Each day brought on new challenges but each day I saw my kids smile more than they had in the past twelve months. Experiencing their joy and hearing their laughs meant more to me than worrying about myself and what others thought of me. I was on a mission of moving forward although the outcome was blurry and daily I had to fight through my emotions I knew deep down inside my tomorrow was finally coming.

My children had an opportunity to meet and reunite with their siblings. I have to give credit to my in-laws because they made sure that regardless of the poor decisions we made as adults, these children deserved the right to have a relationship with one another without boundaries. My in-laws created a safe environment for all the kids. Although my ex and I decided to proceed with the divorce I was secure in knowing that my boys would grow up feeling loved by both families. This definitely wasn't a part of our initial plans but it worked.

Chapter Four

NO TURNING BACK

Commit your way to the Lord; trust in him, and he will act. He will bring forth your righteousness as the light, and your justice as the noonday.

Psalm 37:3-6

Sleepless nights and fear gripped by life. I couldn't get my mind to comprehend that where I was now was real and not a dream. I needed to understand that this was reality. If I continued to look back I would never move forward and my life would be on pause. It was time for me to get my life back with God and allow Him to guide me because I felt like a person wearing a blindfold; not sure where I was headed and what I might crash into along the way. I needed to get a handle on my emotions and a perspective of how to manage my life and become a good mother to my boys. I knew this would include establishing a working relationship with my ex and learning to stay calm and not allow my hurt to overtake me, which was very challenging.

The first year back was rough. I had to make a few tough decisions that would impact the rest of our lives. I pondered often what to do, where to live, where to work and worship. I felt lost, confused and scared. Things got so bad that I didn't know if I was coming or going. I had to fight to keep my sanity at times because I frequently experienced losing my mind. Hope wasn't in the forecast, but I had nothing else to hold on to. I daydreamed about living a different life and making it, but I could never get pass the dream. The dreamed seemed real and I wanted to stay there and make life happen. I owned a business, had a beautiful home and the kids were happy the pain I carried for years was gone. But the reality was it was only a daydream and I needed to accept and move on. (can you explain what the dream is?)

I battled mentally about fighting for my marriage knowing the possibility of being successful and happy wasn't going to happen. Since I had no permanent place to live or person to turn to, I thought fighting for my marriage was the best and only option. Quickly, I was reminded why it didn't work and regardless of my emotions at that time I needed to think rationally; this journey wasn't only about me but my family. Frequently, I would make emotional decisions because of my current state but this time I needed to use wisdom and not react off of my emotions and think things through.

After many weary nights and unpredictable days, I decided that moving forward would take me places while turning back to what I was used to would harvest the same results and lead me to a continuous season of disappointments. My life felt like stained glass, tiny broken pieces glued together to create beauty. Although, I didn't have any idea what people really saw when they looked at me, I could only hope they saw a glimpse of beauty. The one thing I know is if you focus on the possibilities and concentrate on how amazing it is when the light shines through the stain glass, it mysteriously takes your eyes away from the cracks and all you can see is a beautiful picture that tells a story of hope.

I would like to say that everything worked as planned when I made that decision to move forward, but it didn't. I continued to struggle with my emotions. I hated myself at times and felt guilty over and over again for not trying hard enough to make my marriage work. I felt as though I cheated my boys out of a life by denying them the chance to have a two-parent home and that they would grow up and hate me for not trying harder. My thoughts expanded daily with guilt and self-pity that over took me at times. I would try to progress and concentrate on what was important at that moment but as usual I failed. I tried to trick myself and force my heart to react differently by saying to others "Oh, yes I'm fine, we are ok" knowing I wanted to burst out with a loud scream and yell to the top of my lungs with anger, but I knew I would frighten my boys and others.

One evening I was in a place of enough is enough and I decided I needed to have a personal encounter with God. So I fell on my knees and begged God to listen and respond. I remember crying out as though I was a child who felt abandoned by their parent. I was able to release everything in my heart even asking God to forgive me for my wrong actions and lack of faith. Just as a caring mother who rescue her hurting child from a destitute situation, my God rescued me and laid me on His bosom for comfort and assurance that He loved me and had a plan for my life. At that moment my trust factor with God was no longer a problem, He became my Jehovah Shammah "The Lord who is present".

As I said before, things didn't instantly fall in place like the fairy tale. They gradually settled, and I could see the Father's hand manifesting in my life. I remember letting out a big sigh of relief, knowing that life was going forward. I felt myself thinking clearer, feeling better and soon doing better. I was bound for victory, no more guilt, pain, defeat or sadness. It was now time for me to hold fast and trust God with all I had. Considering I had lost everything, giving my will and trust over to Him was easy because I could only climb up the mountain, as I stood at the bottom with no other place to go.

I soon grabbed hold of my faith in God and proceeded to move forward with an expectation that tomorrow would bring me joy and the day after would be even better. Each day was a process and each moment was an experience that would bring change. My attitude had to be adjusted and the way I thought about myself and the future was on the rise. Slowly I could feel my frown flipping and my tears drying. Brighter days were ahead of me. My future looked lively and my past was fading like a stain in clothes after a good washing. God was washing my blemished life and spraying me with His word and love that removes the hardest stains. He had to pretreat me several times because my stains were deeply rooted and scrubbing them was not effective.

After a few dips in cold pretreated water and overnight soaking, all the stains had disappeared. I was reminded that although sometimes we can no longer see the stains with the naked eye there may be residue lingering. I was reminded through the word that I needed to be careful and to give myself a good washing every few days, to prevent the stains from returning. I learned the power of prayer, confessing my sins, asking for forgiveness and reading my word and this kept me clean. Each day brought new hope and my nights no longer frightened me. I could sleep without waking up in night sweats. My children were adjusting and growing fast. Just like the word says in Psalm 30:5 "Weeping may endure for a night, but joy cometh in the morning." My morning had finally arrived.

While my mornings brought sunshine, I had to learn how to depend on God for all my needs. I recall a time when I needed to buy food and pull ups. I had to make a tough decision because I only had $20 and it wasn't enough to do both and barely enough to take care of one of our needs. So I made the decision to buy a few groceries and go to the thrift store and buy used training pants for my son. I remember sitting him down on the potty to have a discussion about potty training and how mommy didn't have any money and I needed him to concentrate and help me out. It didn't work but I learned to make do with what we had and keep it moving.

Nevertheless, things kept coming up but I had a made-up mind that turning back was not an option. Being creative and hustling to make ends meet for my family became the norm for a few months. I had two degrees under my belt and I knew somehow I could make things happen. I starting doing business with a few friends who than introduce me to more friends and God began providing and I really saw the light this time and for once in a very long time I felt good about what tomorrow held for us.

Chapter Five

VICTORY IS MINE

Then you will call upon me and come and pray to me, and I will listen to you.

Jeremiah 29:12

About 27 months after my separation and losing everything, I found myself with hope again. I moved into a new home, had a new job, new friends and a church home. I was on the road to recovery and stability. I was so excited about moving into our new home and grateful to God for all the many blessings He had given us. The day we moved was a Sunday. I borrowed a friend's van and I transported our clothes and a few toys and one air mattress from my mother's house to my new home. It was beautiful, we had two bedrooms, nice open living room, dining room and kitchen overlooking a huge backyard, with a large basement for the boys to run and play all day. We unpacked and set up my room with the one air mattress to share, left our clothes neatly packed in boxes in each room because we had no dressers or hangers. Although we were limited on items the abundance of His love for us out weighed what was lacking.

Less than two hours of us enjoying our new home I received a call, we were asked to supply our address. Moments later a moving truck pulled up to our front door. We were greeted with furniture for the entire house including the basement and patio. Standing in awe I began crying and asking them, "why are you doing this for us." They simply replied, "We had a few items we needed to part from and wanted you to have them." Their humble hearts filled our home with beautiful furniture and love. They hung pictures on the wall and installed ceiling fans and asked if we needed anything else. Choking on my words of unbelief I could barely comprehend what had just happened. In all my years I've never experienced such kindness before. I was so overwhelmed with everything going on I stood in the middle of the floor weeping with joy because God provided in abundance for my family.

The day continued to get even more interesting I received more calls from friends who were cleaning out their garages and wanted to bless our family this particular Sunday. I wondered if I had missed the memo that this Sunday was house cleaning day and for everyone to give their unwanted and precious household items to my family. Talk about feeling loved when love had been so hard for me over the years. I must admit I felt a certain kind of way because I wasn't accustomed to people giving to me in this way. Usually when I would receive a "gift" it meant I must return the favor because their giving was conditional. I paused for a moment waiting for the phone to ring or an unexpected visit from those who gave asking something of me. It didn't happen so I waited a little more and still nothing. I slowly embraced the gifts and outwardly thanked my Father for loving me the way He did.

A few weeks went by and the boys and I were getting settled and the overflow of blessings continued to pour in. This time it was even more interesting than before. My new babysitter offered to give me her bedroom set because her husband despised the color; it was a pink marble oversized set with mirror and lights. It was unique but I loved all twelve pieces of it. After sleeping on an air mattress for two years and living out of boxes, the most unusual designs are pleasant to the eye and can become fascinating and desirable all at once. While loading the truck to bring my new bedroom set home, God did it again. A resident in the community drove by and asked if I wanted an entertainment center, it was brand new and sitting in his drive way just a few houses down. His wife decided she wanted a wall unit instead and they no longer had use for the entertainment center. Yet again I was overwhelmed by His blessings.

Early one morning as I was reminiscing on all the amazing blessings and how quickly He provided for my family, all while feeling undeserving of it all, I heard God speak. I closed my eyes and prepared my heart because although I was blessed in a material way I was still struggling emotionally. I heard The Lord say this would be a season of outpouring unto me and not just materialistically but healing, teaching and forgiveness would manifest in my life and home. God knew I was still broken and angry from my past so He had to create an intervention. It was necessary in where He was taking me. I could not fully understand what all needed to take place or how, but I knew it would happen. I understood that my spiritual house needed to be furnished as nicely as my natural one. Although I found things were looking better for me on my new journey, occasionally I would find myself feeling burdened and trapped. I wanted freedom, but managing my actions, reactions and words was still a struggle. I was determined that this time failure was not an option, and I needed to do things differently. I started to increase my prayer life while learning how to allow God to lead my family.

When I made the decision to allow God to be God and lead us I wanted to see instant change. It wasn't easy waiting because I felt God was moving too slow. I knew His plans were greater than my own, but I had plans on how I wanted to progress. I thought I could fix it and every time I tried I made a step backwards. After about a year of this tug of war I was having with God, I realized that I wasn't going to win. He was stronger and knew more than me. The healing process couldn't take place because I was in the way. I kept blocking God with my selfish ways, ideas, wants and thoughts. He could not reach me because I wouldn't draw near without trying to control things.

In order to reach the stars, I needed to change my way of thinking. I knew I had a lot to learn and a lot to let go. My future began to look bright and my boys' eyes began to sparkle with hope. I felt that I had finally reached a peak in my life where the rainbow was visible and my challenges were no longer my enemy but my strength. I could breathe, I could feel His love, and I could win this battle without a fatal ending. The enemy no longer controlled my destiny. The pain may have held me back for a moment, but the power God gave me I was now able to rebuke and regain.

Victory never looked so promising, but it was obtainable for the first time in a long time and I was going to get it. I was reminded of the old hymn we would sing when I was a child, *"Victory is mine, victory is mine, victory today is mine. I told Satan to get thee behind, victory today is mine"*. Those words rang like bells in my ears and for the first time ever; I understood exactly what that song meant. They became more than just words or harmony to me, they became my victory chant. Over and over in my head I sang that song. I walked those verses and I proclaimed my victory.

No longer did I stand on the battlefield defeated. I was fully clothed and ready for battle, ready to take the enemy down. I didn't know what to expect in the days ahead, except that whatever I was faced with, I was equipped to handle it all. Learning to live this way was a bit unique for me and I realized that not only was my mind being transformed but my words and actions also. Everything needed to line up together so my fight would be effective.

I was never a fighter growing up; my sister always fought my battles, even when I initiated them. Now I was forced to learn how to duke it out with the devil. The only difference between now and my childhood is that when I couldn't find my sister I would run home, but now I could just call on Jesus and the battle was won. I'm still not a big fighter and would prefer just walking away, but in some cases kicking butt is required to get victory.

The right training camp positions you to be victorious in a battle. Even the scariest person can win a battle with good coaching, equipment, dedication and a renewed mindset. The battlefield is the place where the battle is fought. For you it could be your mind, body or spirit, but regardless of where it is, you can win and be victorious. The bible says in Deuteronomy 20:4 (NKJV) *"For the Lord your God is He who goes with you to fight for you against your enemies, to give you the victory."* He is my coach and protector so I trust in Him.

Each morning I prepared myself for the battlefield because I had no idea what or where I would be fighting on that day. Many times I would drive to work talking with the Lord in my heavenly language because words couldn't express what my spirit yearned for. I needed the Holy Spirit to intercede to the Father on my behalf and to give me the strength to deal with whatever was coming my way. On other days, I would just weep because like before, words could not express my pain. Many times they were not tears of defeat, but tears that expressed joyful pain (pains that birth miracles) when you realized that only God could do something that you had no power to do especially when the outcome should have been different.

The more I settled into my new season, the more I could see a stream of light breaking through the clouds over my family. The gap that separated me from my future was slowly closing and the sunshine gently rested on us like the dew in the morning. It felt so good to see darkness pass over me and to feel the embrace of comfort and gentleness fall like autumn leaves.

My eyes could close without fear or fear of what I would see looking back at me. Victory became a part of my day. My boys were happy and I could not imagine being anywhere else in life at that moment but where I was. I had finally learned and understood that the battle is not mine but the Lord's. Again I chant what brought me through *"Victory is mine, victory is mine, victory today is mine. I told Satan to get thee behind victory today is mine."* I stand on the battle waving my banner of victory.

Chapter Six

MY FORGIVENESS CAMPAIGN

"Blessed is the man who trusts in the LORD And whose trust is the LORD. "For he will be like a tree planted by the water, that extends its roots by a stream And will not fear when the heat comes; But its leaves will be green, And it will not be anxious in a year of drought Nor cease to yield fruit.

Jeremiah 17:7-8

Tomorrow had finally arrived. My life was forming into the plan God had designed. I felt the horror of the rollercoaster ride of my past descending from its last drop coasting to the platform called the finish line. My tears of pain no longer consumed my day and the panic of my heart no longer beat twice but just once with a calming beat of peace that only God could provide. I could hear the tone of my breath with a sigh of relief inhaling victory that the enemy tried to steal from me. The palms of my hands no longer sweat with fear but were dry with a clasp to hold tight His promises that were now near.

I remember holding my head up high as if it was trying to discover something new but in reality I wanted to keep my eyes on the prize. For years I held my head down regretting every decision I had made and all I could recall was the track of dirt and residue that entangled my thoughts and progress. Freedom seemed closer than ever before because I learned to trust my Creator. I was living a different life for the first time in years. A life filled with joy, peace, hope, and love, but soon I realized that I still needed to walk in forgiveness. I had to learn to release the pain that had captured me all these years that made bondage so common.

Forgiving those who have crushed me, spit on me

and wished me nothing but death reminded me of Joseph and how he embraced his brothers by letting go of the past. I had to turn off all negative thoughts and take on the mind of Christ and approach each situation uniquely understanding each reaction would be different but the way I would respond mattered the most. Over the course of years, I managed to reach way back in my past, all the way to my childhood and uncover scars that left me bruised. I remember facing one abuser with tears streaming down my face asking why me, why did you choose to hurt me? After spending time with him we hugged and I forgave him. Don't get me wrong that was one of the hardest things I have ever done in my life, but it was also one of the most memorable moments I have ever had. I walked away realizing that it is easier to forgive than to walk in anger; you spend less time on why you're mad and more time thinking about the next person to forgive.

My forgiveness campaign carried on and even to this day I find time to forgive and ask for forgiveness because it's imperative for my growth and how I parent my children. I can't teach my children one thing and live another way. I searched my heart constantly revealing those pains I had buried for years. Some were too painful to unveil at that moment so I put those aside with prayer hoping later I could embrace it and forgive. My baby steps became bigger steps, then skips, and then hopping and eventually I ran. Forgiveness is the master key that opens doors of unlimited possibilities. The bible says in Matthew 6:14-15 (KJV) *"For if you forgive men when they sin against you, your heavenly Father will also forgive you. But if you do not forgive men their sins, your Father will not forgive your sins."*

I remember one incident I had where this person abused me verbally, mentally and financially for years. I would have nightmares, fears and anxiety attacks because of the abuse. I struggled to trust others and expected them to all turn evil eventually because that the experience I was familiar with. The experience was so horrific that I began developing characteristics that was not normal at least to those closest to me. I was tired of the guilt, hurt and pain and knew that I must let this go. Freedom from this type of hurt was a process. I needed to fast, pray, go to counseling and eventually forgive them and myself.

Over the years I have gotten stronger and found myself walking in freedom and sharing my story that assisted others in walking in their freedom. It's a difficult thing when you want to be free but you're not sure how to BE free. When bondage rapes your mind, the stronghold is so intense just thinking clear isn't easy. Until you have truly been captive mentally by a stronghold, understanding the mindset and thought process of others is unpredictable. We always assume people should or could behave differently, but the reality is you don't know what they have endured. So don't expect others to respond like you, just pray. When one has been in a mental stronghold over years, reality to them isn't reality to you.

I would like to say that after I prayed, fasted and had years of counseling and walked in forgiveness, that my life went back to normal with no side effect, but I would be lying. I continued to build upon the process that was put in place because the devil is tricky. What worked for a while eventually stopped working. It's just like an old car. You notice a leak and you take it to the mechanic to get it repaired. You do everything they tell you to do to keep it running properly to add years of life to the car, but the mechanic also instructs you on maintaining the vehicle because it adds even more years and value to the car. Cars that are not maintained eventually die and you have to replace the parts or junk the car. It's the same process for us. You must maintain your life and deliverance though the word of God and prayer and even additional counseling if needed. So when you are fighting through those tough thoughts, pray, press, read and seek out help. Don't allow pride to set you back.

One thing that I do often to keep me on track is putting verses related to my situation in a journal and I read them daily out loud several times. This allows me to fill my spirit with God's word, which brings a positive impact, while removing all negative content from my mind. The more I read the word, the more the word becomes alive and my life reflects what I'm feeding it.

Chapter Seven

BLINDSIDED

"Praise be to the God and Father of our Lord Jesus Christ, the Father of compassion and the God of all comfort, who comforts us in all our troubles, so that we can comfort those in any trouble with the comfort we ourselves receive from God.

2 Cor. 1:3-4

Things were going as planned or at least I thought they were. I was secured finally with a safe home for my children, a steady job and my finances were on the rise. Suddenly I was blindsided. The hit was so hard it threw me right off my feet. My youngest son had been physically abused by another adult that denied the allegations and not only was my son hurting from the abuse but also the lies. He was scared and dealing with the emotional ramification of the abuse. My new life after one year was back in chaos and I didn't know what to do. I felt like a bad mother because I thought the environment was safe but it wasn't. Everyone questioned me and I felt as though I was under investigation for something that was out of my control.

Have you ever felt that all your good, backed fired when you were giving your best and life felt unfair? Well right at that moment that was me and how I felt. Wondering, how could things seem so perfect be perfectly wrong. I beat myself up and questioned if I had missed the signs with the hustle and bustle of my life. I was trying so hard to be a flawless mother making the right decisions for my family and just like that an unexpected accident happened. How was I going to teach my son to trust again better yet how was I going to trust the next person who smiles in my face and not know the intensions of their heart. This was a mountain that needed to be conquered in our life and I didn't feel adequate to properly climb without the fear of what if or what's next.

After several childcare placements and watching my child struggle with acceptance, trust and fear, I knew that therapy and prayer was the appropriate intervention at that time. Not long after the incident God sent us an angel in the form of a sweet senior citizen with a warm heart, soft tone and lots of love. The next three years my kids were embraced by this family and we eventually adopted her as our Grandmother. She was perfect and the best thing that happened to us in a long time. I was able to rest at night and work during the day knowing that my children were safe.

We continued to deal with the effects of the abuse as my son grew and started kindergarten. We struggled year after year with teachers until I was introduced to an alternative learning environment for my son at a therapeutic school. It took some coaching to get me on board but my dear friend who is an advocate for children, worked with me to ensure me that this was the best and most appropriate placement for my son. This school was equipped with everything necessary to help my son succeed and help our family move forward. No parent wants to imagine anything bad happening to their children when you put them in the care of others. This incident caused me to be on alert at all times because the safety of my children was priority and protecting them was my duty. I put down my guard and allowed this new system to work for our family.

After the placement of my son and relocating closer to my employer, I was now challenged with leaving our caregiver and finding someone new. This in and of itself brought on a new anxiety because we had finally jumped over the hurtle with placement and now I needed to find a new caregiver for before and after school care. I knew that too much change at once would be overwhelming for us but being a single parent I had no choice because I had no help. We went through four nannies in one year. We experienced unskilled help, inappropriate tones, lack of commitment and the list goes on and on.

Nanny number five was great! She shared her responsibilities with her daughter and they would alternate every other week. They were an amazing duo from Jamaica. They were highly recommended, loving and very supportive of our needs. I allowed the mother to occupy my bedroom because I wanted her to be comfortable because she was up in age, so I slept in the bottom bunk of my kid's beds. They cooked, cleaned and loved my children as their own. We even got to experience a few Caribbean dishes. After several months my duo's situations changed and they could no longer care for my children; years later my children and I still find it enjoyable reminiscing about having them in our lives.

I found it tough being back to square one but this time it was different I had to depend on an agency to select the right person for our family. For the next 8 months we managed to get through the school year with a consistent provider. Although we disagreed on many things, we learned how to respect one another's opinions and stay focus on the purpose at hand. I have a very conservative but firm way of discipline and a strict set of rules in my home. Many times my nanny didn't always agree. However, a friendly reminder from me kept things on track because at the end of the day her responsibility was to care for the boys and not judge my parenting. Once we managed to get over our differences in parenting my home was at peace and the boys enjoyed her adventure nature and care she provided.

After seven months and the end of the school year my nanny and I decided to part ways. Yes, once again I was feeling overwhelmed and searching for more resources and assistance with the boys. Night after night, I worried about tomorrow I was exhausted from the stress of my job and home and I felt like a failure. Everyone around me was saying the same thing, "It will get better, hang in there". The more I heard those words with the intent to comfort me, the angrier I became because I felt alone, defeated and drained. I felt like no one understood my dilemma and looking in from the outside didn't share the true story of my struggles. How dare they compare my life to theirs or tell me it's going to get better while I'm drowning. Each day I grew angry and wanted to just walk away from it all. However, I knew that I had two responsibilities that required my full attention. I managed to put things back into perspective and kept pressing.

God began dealing with me and reminding me of His promises. Although, I felt confused because I thought I was living right, doing right, going to church, paying my tithes and offerings, helping those in need and loving my kids, what more was necessary to live a good life? I watched people and families around me living happy and comfortable and not even doing half of what I was doing for the Lord. So, I thought why is He punishing me? I could think of many sins and wrongs I have done over my lifetime and maybe it was payback time. I was not perfect in any way and I had lived a full life of sin in my past, so I figured it all had finally caught up to me and now I must pay for what I had done. I was totally wrong. God had a plan for me even through this trial. It wasn't about punishing me but more about strengthening me.

Right in the midst of my contemplating walking off my job and staying home with my children because I had run out of resources, God released an emergency 911 call on my behalf to my neighbors. They all knew my struggle and together they decided to give me a hand and help with my children. I had one single women care for them for a few months and then two families helped after that. Even the rental office employees joined in and helped with the kids. I learned that it truly does take a village to raise a child and the village helped us. Without the support of my village, I would not have known what to do. Seeing beyond my circumstances didn't seem possible. I felt that I had hit a point in my life of no return. Only God could have created a blessing out of nothing. I had absolutely no options visible to the naked eyes. This experience proved to me that all things are possible through Christ.

I could see the sunshine bursting through the

clouds for us again. Things were changing, and I was expecting newness because everything I had endured over the years with my sons brought me to my knees and gave me a praise no man could steal. I was on a high for Jesus, with gratitude on my lips thanking Him for every blessing and seeking the next opportunity that deserved His praise. Just as quickly as I murmured those words, my atmosphere shifted swiftly. God proved to me that He was my provider and everything I needed He had.

Chapter Eight

A GIFT FROM GOD

"From now on, every generation will call me blessed! For he, the Mighty One, is holy, and he has done great things for me. He shows mercy from generation to generation to all who fear him."

Luke 1:48b-50

Right in the midst of my praise from the most hectic time in my life, God gave me another child. This child was special. She entered my world through a spiritual assignment. Although I didn't physically birth her, she was divinely appointed to our family. I was given the assignment to love this broken and fragile girl as my own. She was sixteen and needed love and care. I was in shock; even disbelief because of everything I had endured with the boys as a single parent God couldn't be adding to my family. I prayed to God and reminded him of my situation and that times were a little tough and I wasn't quite sure if He meant to call my name or a name similar to mine like Laverne or Latrice or something. I was certain that He clearly made a mistake.

It happened on October 1, 2007, I was traveling to Detroit, MI on a business trip departing out of Chicago O'Hare Airport. As I was preparing to enter through security a young lady headed in the opposite direction wearing an airport employee uniform passed me with a smile and I smiled back and continued to proceed through security. As I approached security, God whispered to me "She will be significant in your life." I looked around because I had never experienced anything like that before. I chuckled because I thought I was having an insane moment but really I was trying to get my thoughts back on track. Here I was walking through an airport minding my own business and God allowed someone to cross my path and gives me an assignment. Shaking my head I proceeded through security with no additional thought about what just happened.

I finally reached my designated terminal; it was packed and standing room only. I heard an announcement that our flight was currently delayed. There was no bad weather in Illinois or Michigan so it was unclear what the issue was. With no seats available at my terminal I started looking around and notice that the terminal diagonal from mine had plenty of available seats so I proceeded to the other side. As I sat down and gather my belongings I looked up and there she was sitting right in front of me. I was in shock because I thought to myself I must be losing it. So I adjusted myself in my seat and blinked my eyes a few times and she was still there. I thought to myself is this really happening, what does God want me to say or do? After about five minutes I smiled, she smiled and I felt even sillier than before. Then I heard The Lord say "just start talking and I'll do the rest" I'm thinking just start talking this has to be the most uncomfortable thing I've ever done. I was literally freaking out because I thought this girl is going to think I'm crazy and may scream "stranger danger" or something.

I got up enough nerves and said "Excuse me can you please find out why my flight is delayed?" she reply "Sure, one moment". She walked away and I wanted to run away but God would not allow me to move. It was like my legs were locked in place. The young lady returned and said "There's a problem with the incoming flight from Canada, you should be boarding in a couple of hours". I then introduced myself and we began chatting while I waited for my flight. She shared her life with me and my heart began embracing her. I can't really explain it in details because it happened in a supernatural way. I gave her my business card and said "If you need someone to talk to about college or anything let me know". I soon departed for my flight and prayed all the way to Detroit because I really wanted to know what God wanted from me. I knew personally or financially I had nothing to give her. After three days of attending the conference in Detroit, I dismissed what happened between me and the young lady and I proceeded to my daily routine thinking that maybe I had imagined all of this considering this was a new experience for me.

A few days later while at work I received a call. It was her. She asked about my trip and wanted to know

when we could meet and talk more. I had no idea
what all God wanted to do with this but I was willing
to allow Him to intervene because it was obvious He'd
brought us together. We both approached this
relationship with caution because our lives were a
reflection of our brokenness. One call led to another,
one visit led to another and before we knew it God had
blossomed our encounter into something more
beautiful than words could ever express. This young
lady had become a part of my life, a family member
and daughter so quickly. She learned to trust me and I
learned to love again. Who knew that God would take
two complete strangers with similar backgrounds and
prosper a family? We both learned that family doesn't
have to be blood but a bond.

As we allowed God to continue to knit our hearts
together it was always hard to explain to others how
we met. I can confess it was uncomfortable at times
sharing our story especially to non-believers because
they thought it was weird. I think we both struggled
with introducing each other to our family and friends
because in their eyes, this just wasn't normal and
everyone knew our past and they would get defensive.
Nonetheless, to our surprise everything fell into place
and no questions were asked, my family accepted her
and vice versa. My boys had a big sister and accepted

her immediately. She became my daughter and we learned how to love and heal one another through our experiences, loses, fears and troubles. She accepted me for me and I did the same for her. Quickly she adapted to my family and became one of the kids. I did question God a few times because things changed and I wasn't sure what the outcome would be.

I was able to experience life's big moments with her as she transitioned from high school to college and then off to cosmetology school. She and I became friends and family. We laughed and cried with one another but mostly we learned to love deeply, although we were both a bit unsure of what the future held for us, we continued to press without boundaries. I would like to say we had the best relationship but I would not be telling the truth. We fought, disagreed, played the silent game a few times but not once would God allow us to walk away completely. I quickly learned the ups and downs with teenagers and the independent attitude once they reach 18 but nevertheless she prepared me for the two coming behind her.

My fondest memory is when we had our very first mommy and daughter weekend. We drove to St. Louis for my dear friend's graduation. It was Mother's Day weekend and just the two of us on the open road with music and good conversation. Driving down I-55 we talked about us and how much we had grown and what our future looked like and what we wanted to do in the next couple of years and if we would marry. Yes, we talked about having significant others. She asked me to promise to let her help match me with someone so her step-dad would be amazing and she promised me to let me drill her future as well because I wanted what was best for her. We found ourselves sharing secrets, fears, disappointments and hard times for the first time ever. I even opened up about my childhood and all the things I wanted to become and the dreams that were deferred; how much I was so grateful to have her in my life.

After 5 hours of driving and eating our favorite meal together, chicken wings, talking about everything imaginable our bond grew stronger and it was no longer a question about why God did what He did. He knew we needed one another, He knew that I was just right for her and she was just right for me. He knew that no one else could do what she had done for me and what I had done for her. She had become my baby girl and what I thought this weekend was going to be like, was greater than my expectation. I got to show her off to my college friend and her family and she fit right in. They adored her and she instantly had an extended family.

The weekend continued to bring surprises as we shopped and laughed. On the morning of Mother's day she laid a card on my bed and the words inside crafted my heart to a deeper place. I cried and hugged my sweet daughter and embraced that moment because I wanted it to last forever. I finally knew she loved me as much as I loved her. I thought for a moment what would my life have been like if God hadn't sent her to me. I was persuaded that it wasn't about what I could do for her but more about what she has done for me.

When I think about her and what she means to me it's really difficult to express to others because words truly will never capture what my heart feels. She is my inspiration when things get tough. I think about her life and what God has done for her and through her and I am inspired to keep it moving. She has shown me how to stretch and believe the impossible and that no matter how often we may not agree, our hearts are connected for this purpose. We would have never thought many years ago that what we are experiencing now is what God had intended. I am so glad that God brought us together at the most vulnerable times in our lives, so that we could learn how to forget our own pains and troubles and love someone who hurt a little more than ourselves.

Chapter Nine

A PRAYING SINGLE MOTHER

Devote yourselves to prayer, being watchful and thankful. – Col. 4:2

Over the years, I watched the boys grow emotionally through their experiences from many highs and lows. The boys occasionally dealt with nights of tears, rejection and pain that developed from the separation of their father. I knew that I didn't always have the right words to bring them comfort, so I prayed. I would cry out so loud to God to protect their tiny hearts from a giant situation that had the possibility of growing out of control. I could not sit back and watch their hearts break from every disappointment or broken promise. As their mother, I needed to teach them to pray, not only for themselves but also for their father. It's not healthy to know what to do and not do it or better yet not train my children to respond in a godly manner. The bible says in Proverbs 22:6 (NKJV) *"Train up a child in the way he should go, And when he is old he will not depart from it."* I didn't have all the right answers but I did know that prayer changes all things.

As time went on, the boys have learned to manage their emotions in a more mature way. I remember times when the hurt was so intense their behaviors reflected their hearts. They didn't know how to express to me what they were feeling verbally so they would act out in ways that didn't match their character. I would like to say I understood immediately but I didn't. So I would really get angry by their behavior and I would respond accordingly. Of course I felt like a bad mom after I realized that they were only displaying their hurt from a previous interaction with their father. The lesson for all of us during this season was communication. I needed the boys to communicate with me their feelings and I needed to listen and help them cope and navigate how to respond.

I started teaching the boys to write letters to their father even if we didn't mail them. I wanted them to have an outlet on how to express their emotions by being truthful to themselves and their father. My thought behind this exercise would not only teach the boys expression, but it gave them an understanding that it was ok to tell a parent when they are affected by their actions in a negative way. We teach our children to express their appreciation when we give to them but we never teach our children to share their feelings of disappointment that we as parents have caused. This exercise was more than effective; it changed the atmosphere in our home. I no longer had to deal with major outburst because the boys learned to channel their emotions and write.

The boys became so skilled at this exercise they decided to take it up a level and began writing poems, lyrics and coordinating music to create songs that reflected what they were feeling. My oldest son is the singer and my youngest has an ear for music so together they would create and share with me. I found it interesting to see God move in a way I would have never imagined. My background is in creative arts so of course I enjoyed watching them perform and even helped them bring more creativity to their acts. Watching and listening to the boys express themselves was incredible. They even began sharing when I had disappointed or hurt them. I was now getting a better understanding on how to discipline and encourage the boys as they grew older.

To see how far the boys have grown and developed is a praise report alone. My eldest prince was once very bitter, angry, broken and competitive while also being very influenced by others; he lacked self-confidence. I was told that his areas of opportunity were most likely to have developed over time from rejection and the absence of his father. He went through a period of being defiant and I felt challenged daily dealing with his rebellious behavior. He thought I was the only cause of him not seeing his father and the struggle continued. Once we put a plan in place to help him he improved and grew. No longer did we struggle with him blaming me, he understood and knew the truth. Slowly as he developed and learned to managed his emotions though writing, counseling, prayer and mentorship we began to see exactly who God said he was he was- an incredible, talented, God-fearing young man.

My youngest prince was pierced with fear, low self-esteem, rejection and depression. I worried mostly about his development overall. He got a bad reputation early in life and I didn't want him to become a statistic. We built a community of supporters to help him progress in a manner that worked best with his experiences. I didn't want him labeled, so I worked diligently to secure his confidence and we focused on his strengths and passion for sports and serving others. As we continued on the path God chose for him, I watched him overcome damaging obstacles. Daily, I watched him develop into a young man with dreams, compassion for others and missions.

Without God's guidance and the support of others, our lives would be different today. It's so important to trust God because when all else fails God reigns. I never imagined living this life and I never wanted my children to go through as much as they have. Although we cannot change the past, we do have the ability to design our futures if we only believe.

CHAPTER TEN

I AM DIVINE

You intended to harm me, but God intended it all for good. He brought me to this position so I could save the lives of many people.

Genesis 50:20

To God be the glory because of His love and faithfulness to my family. God brought us through the most difficult times in our lives that were once so dark and dreary. When I think about how I once felt, the world weighed heavy on my shoulders and tomorrow seemed so far away and just getting out of the bed was a task! I could now shout Hallelujah God is good. As I reflect back, I remember those nights I would lay prostrate before the Lord, asking Him to wean me from the dependencies of the government, family and friends and to mend my brokenness. I sought God for direction to teach me step by step how to raise my family. I didn't want to play both roles, I only wanted to do what I was equipped to do and I wanted to do it to the best of my ability that would make a positive impact in my children's lives. I wanted and needed God to permeate my entire being so that I could let go and trust Him.

As I allowed God to take control, my darkest nights brightened over time. I saw my life lining up with the word of God and I saw God as the head of our family. I still wasn't quite sure what my purpose in life would become, but I knew He had a plan. He saved me from me and saved my children from destruction, so if He could do it for me He can do it for anyone. My life compared to this world was tiny and my problems didn't match too many single mothers but my pain and struggles were real. I learned an important lesson, and that lesson I learned was true and has changed my life forever. The bible says in Psalm 68:5 *"Father to the fatherless, defender of widows--this is God, whose dwelling is holy."* That alone changed the course of my family. God kept His promise to us.

So as I thought I was raising a prince without a king and a family without a head I was truly mistaken. From the beginning God was with us. He guided my life, taught me how to make the right choices, counseled me when I felt overwhelmed and proved daily while assuring me that I was never alone. Trusting Him became the only way to have a life of peace and comfort. Only God could give me the blue print to raising a prince without a king and only God can make promises that are never broken. We may not have a tangible king in our home, but we indeed have the help from the King of all kings.

Everything that happened and every experience I have had brought me to the place of humility. I can now rejoice without fear and love without worry. You never know how strong you are until you are faced with circumstances that seem to overrule your ability to stand and fight. It's not how tough you are during the fight or what skills you think you have or how powerful your roar is, but it's about how you fight. I'm reminded of when I was a child and my sister who is only 13 months older than me fought every day after school and sometimes even on the weekends. She wasn't a skillful fighter but she sent the message to her component that she will fight until she wins. So when we are faced with a challenge that requires you to fight be like my sister and fight until you win. Don't allow your roar to be bigger than your punch, fight with purpose and come out a winner.

Through my trials I won because God created something bigger and greater than I could ever imagine. He took the most miserable times in my life and created a ministry. This fight wasn't about me but about the billion single parents left to raise their children along. I wasn't special just a vessel He used to bring glory to Himself. God took the thing that almost destroyed me to give hope and life to the lifeless. In January 2009, Praying Single Mothers was founded to inspire and equip single mothers around the nation to soar through their situations.

This platform created an opportunity for me to work with and serve single mothers and their families for the last six years by providing resources and an outlet to pull them up and out. My heart is filled with love and honor to have worked with women who are making a difference not only in their families but within their communities. I salute you mothers for allowing God to use PSM and me to empower, restore and equip each of you.

In October 2014, Praying Single Mothers became PSM for Single Parents; we've expanded our reach so that not one single parent is left behind. Reaching single fathers has become an exciting extension for us. Our mission is to empower, restore, and equip single parent families by providing professional services and mentoring opportunities via conferences, workshops, seminars, and trainings. PSM will leverage its community network to enable and provide resources to single parent families allowing them to maintain a holistic life while raising their children, our future.

Single Parents, when you feel defeated, remember these words

"I AM DIVINE D-I-V-I-N-E".

I am divine D-I-V-I-N-E.
The day of my conception God hand knitted me in my mother's womb. He knew the plan for my life even when my mother had no clue. First, He named me destiny when He blew His breath into my lungs and then allowed my mother to cradle me in her arms. She looked me in my eyes and whispered my name not knowing my life would be filled with so much pain

I am divine D-I-V-I-N-E
Wonderfully made even in His image, I am His creation on this earth with a mission. You may look at me knowing a little or a lot about my past, but Haggai 2:9 says *"The glory of this latter temple shall be greater than my past"*. So don't judge me by what you know but love me because the bible says so.

I am divine D-I-V-I-N-E
I sometimes walk as if the weight of the world is heavy on my back. Not trusting anyone, my faith in people is in lack. So I have to fall on my knees asking God

please heal my heart so you may impart. That I may embrace true love the way you gave the love of your life that I may be saved.

I am divine D-I-V-I-N-E
Sometimes when my head is hanging low and my butt is dragging behind; I can still hear the Lord whisper my name promising, now is the time for me to reign. Suddenly I realize my life is in His hands. So I respond by saying "Lord I'm stepping out and trusting you I can."

I am divine D-I-V-I-N-E
Most days I struggled but my children were fed and I did whatever it took to keep a roof over their heads. I remember losing my job, even my car. I turned to the state to assist when the people I depended on clearly resist. That's when I knew something had to give, I needed to change my perspective and cry out, Jesus Your will.

I am divine D-I-V-I-N-E
I tell you today humble as a child that I thank God for every opportunity not trying to draw a crowd. I just want to pour out my heart to all whom I meet, telling them about my Lord and that their journey won't be a

defeat. My heart is filled with passion for you. Hold your heads up and repeat after me...

I am divine D-I-V-I-N-E.

Mother, Mentor, Minister, and Motivator the M's that navigate LaVeda M. Jones' life for success. LaVeda M. Jones is a native of Mobile, Alabama and a longtime resident of the Chicago Metropolitan community. As a divorced parent, LaVeda discovered that many single parents were in need of additional resources in order to navigate the complexities of parenting. LaVeda is the Founder of (PSM) Professional Services and Mentoring for Single Parents, Nfp™ a global non-profit organization and unified voice of single parent families.

As the visionary of PSM, LaVeda has helped develop a platform where like-minded parents around the globe can come together in one place to gather resources, share stories, learn, be mentored and bridge the gap of feeling alone. PSM is known in communities for being an organization that is engaged and passionate about single parents and their families. Nobody understands the life of single parenting as well as those who are single parents or were single parents.

With a lifelong passion for the arts, LaVeda holds a Bachelor of Fine Arts from the International Academy of Design and Technology. In keeping with her love for art and children, LaVeda spent ten years as a teacher and owner of Make It Art Design, Inc. where she specialized in small business creative development.

LaVeda M. Jones has a heart for people and is a leader known for her gift of servant leadership, which she has put to use serving a number of ministries in the past 22 years. LaVeda also serves as a Board Member of Loving Arms Youth Foundation.

Contact Information:
Email: ljones@psmforsingleparents.org

847-220-8061

LaVeda Jones

P.O. Box 126

Grayslake, IL 60030

Social Media:
www.twitter.com/LavedaJones

www.facebook.com/authorlavedajones

PSM Contact information:

www.psmforsingleparents.org

https://www.facebook.com/PSMforsingleparents

https://twitter.com/psmsingleparent

866-556-5561

19468338R00057

Made in the USA
San Bernardino, CA
28 February 2015